I0824268

Christmas

Holidays around the World

Katie Gillespie

LIGHTBOX
openlightbox.com

LIGHTBOX

Go to **www.openlightbox.com** and enter this book's unique code.

ACCESS CODE

LBXF4836

Lightbox is an all-inclusive digital solution for the teaching and learning of curriculum topics in an original, groundbreaking way. Lightbox is based on National Curriculum Standards.

OPTIMIZED FOR

- ✔ TABLETS
- ✔ WHITEBOARDS
- ✔ COMPUTERS
- ✔ AND MUCH MORE!

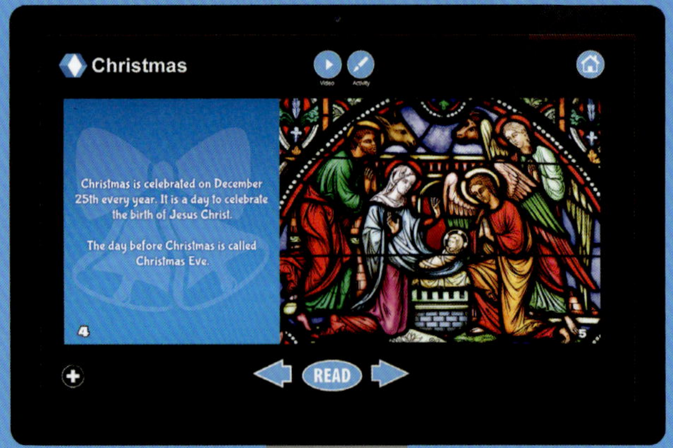

STANDARD FEATURES OF LIGHTBOX

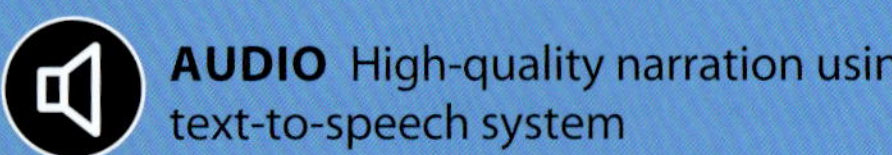
AUDIO High-quality narration using text-to-speech system

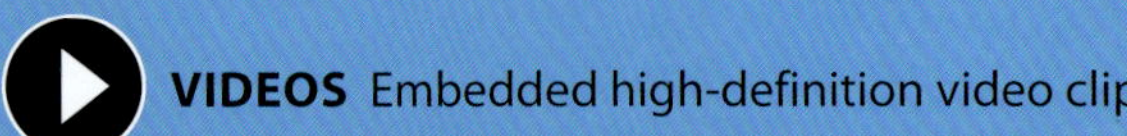
VIDEOS Embedded high-definition video clips

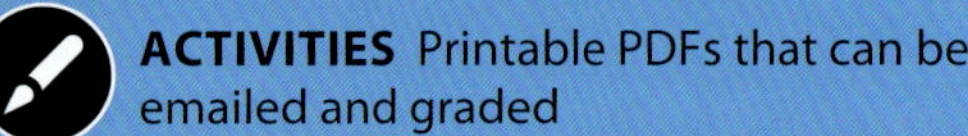
ACTIVITIES Printable PDFs that can be emailed and graded

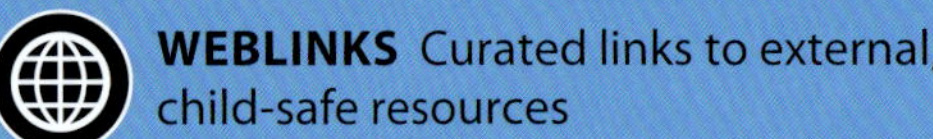
WEBLINKS Curated links to external, child-safe resources

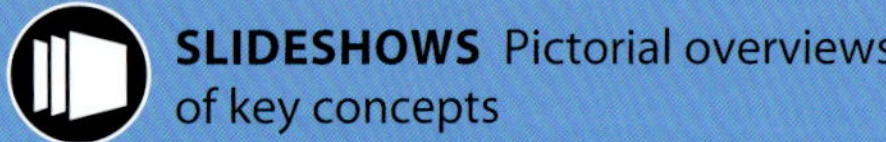
SLIDESHOWS Pictorial overviews of key concepts

INTERACTIVE MAPS Interactive maps and aerial satellite imagery

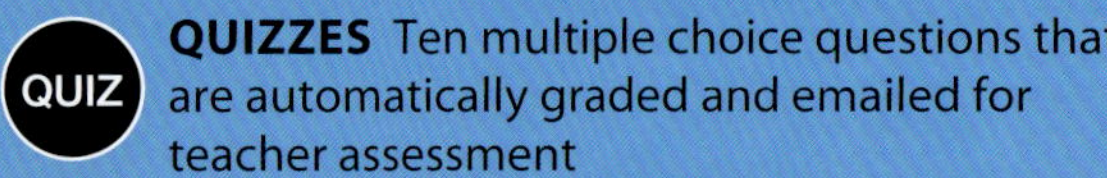
QUIZZES Ten multiple choice questions that are automatically graded and emailed for teacher assessment

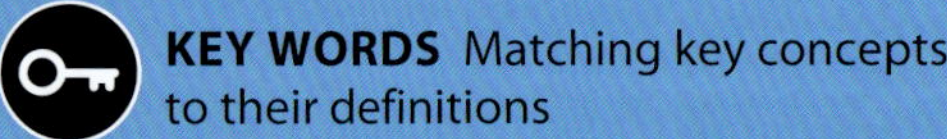
KEY WORDS Matching key concepts to their definitions

VIDEOS

WEBLINKS

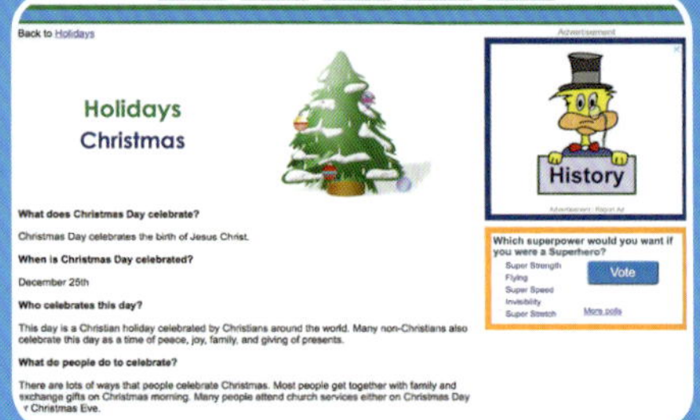

SLIDESHOWS

QUIZZES

Holidays around the world

Christmas

CONTENTS

2 Lightbox Access Code
4 When Is Christmas?
6 What Is Christmas?
8 Santa Claus
10 Where We Celebrate
12 Coming Together
14 How We Celebrate
16 More Traditions
18 Helping Others
20 Special Celebrations
22 Christmas Facts
24 Key Words

Christmas is celebrated on December 25th every year. It is a day to celebrate the birth of Jesus Christ.

The day before Christmas is called Christmas Eve.

5

Christmas has been celebrated for about **2,000 years.**

Christmas is celebrated by people called Christians. They believe that Jesus was the son of God.

Christmas is not just about Christian customs. The holiday also has traditions from other winter festivals.

Santa Claus plays an important role at Christmastime.

On Christmas Eve, he visits homes around the world and leaves presents for good children.

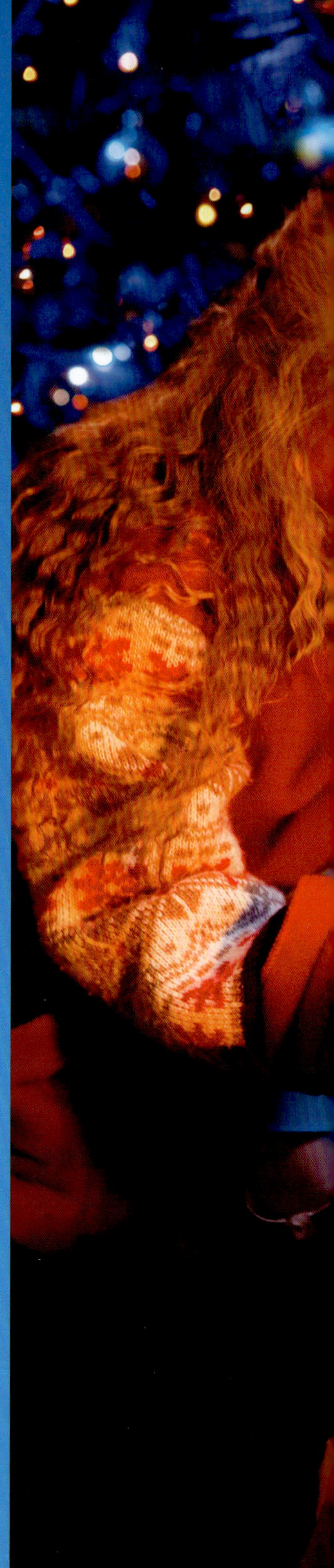

The hopes and fears
Of all the years
Are meet in
Thee tonight

Special church services are held on Christmas Eve. Many other celebrations take place across the world in December.

The **longest-running Christmas parade** in the United States is the **Santa Claus Parade** in Peoria, Illinois.

Christmas is not only a religious holiday. Many people think of Christmas as a chance to spend time with loved ones.

Christmas is a time to eat special foods, such as turkey and stuffing. Families often get together for a traditional meal.

People bake treats such as fruitcake or shortbread cookies at Christmas.

Christmas trees are a popular symbol of the holiday. Trees are decorated with colorful ornaments and bright strands of lights.

The Rockefeller Center Christmas tree in New York City has more than 30,000 lights.

EMERGENCY
EXIT ONLY
ALARM WILL SOUND
EMERGENCY EXIT ONLY
Alarm Will Sound
Pine Street Inn
Ending Homelessness

Christmas is a time to help others. Some people serve food to those in need.

Donations of warm clothing, toys, and other gifts are often made at Christmas.

Special music is played to celebrate the holiday season. People sing joyful songs called carols.

CHRISTMAS FACTS

These pages provide more detail about the interesting facts found in the book. They are intended to be used by adults as a learning support to help young readers round out their knowledge of each holiday featured in the *Holidays around the World* series.

Pages 4–5

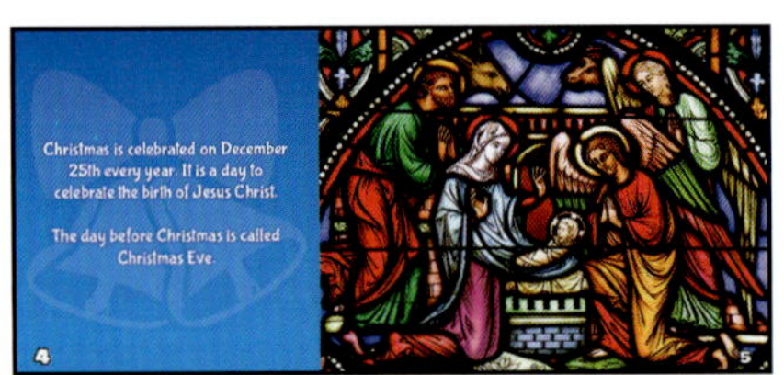

Christmas is celebrated on December 25th every year. The term *Christmas* comes from an Old English phrase meaning "Christ's mass." Although the exact date of Jesus' birth is unknown, it is observed every year on December 25th. Some people believe that this day was chosen because of other festivals that took place around the same time. In Ancient Rome, pagans celebrated the winter solstice on December 17th with a festival called Saturnalia.

Pages 6–7

Christmas has been celebrated for about two thousand years by people called Christians. Today, Christmas incorporates traditions from different festivals around the world. Ancient Romans placed lit candles on trees, as a symbol of Saturn's light, during Saturnalia. Christians began to do the same at Christmas, as a tribute to the star that led the way to the birthplace of Jesus. Common Christmas customs, such as exchanging gifts and sending greeting cards, evolved over time as well.

Pages 8–9

Santa Claus plays an important role at Christmastime. He is said to live at the North Pole with Mrs. Claus and his elves. There, they make toys all year long, to be delivered on Christmas Eve. Santa is a jolly man who wears a bright red hat and suit, trimmed with white fur. He has a sleigh pulled by eight flying reindeer, which is filled with gifts for children around the world. Every year on December 24th, Santa visits each child's home and brings presents down the chimney.

Pages 10–11

Special church services are held on Christmas Eve. Many people attend a ceremony called midnight mass. This special service honors the Christian belief that Jesus was born around midnight. Throughout the month of December, other non-religious celebrations are held, including parties, concerts, and parades. Some places hold festivals of lights or neighborhood decorating contests.

Pages 12–13

Christmas is not only a religious holiday. For many, Christmas is a season of good will and merriment. People take time off from school and work to get together with family and friends. Loved ones often travel to visit and exchange presents with one another. Many families have their own unique traditions at Christmas as well.

Pages 14–15

Christmas is a time to eat special foods, such as turkey and stuffing. In many families, it is tradition to come together for a large meal on Christmas Eve or Christmas Day. While the menu may vary, it often includes homemade treats. Some desserts are elaborately decorated, such as gingerbread houses made with jellybeans, candy canes, and icing.

Pages 16–17

Christmas trees are a popular symbol of the holiday. The practice of decorating Christmas trees began in Germany in the 1600s. A man walking home on Christmas night thought the evergreen trees looked beautiful by starlight. He cut down a small tree and took it home to decorate with candles. Today, trees are topped with stars or angels in honor of Christian beliefs. Gifts are placed under the tree to open on Christmas morning.

Pages 18–19

Christmas is a time to help others. Giving back to the community is an important way to mark the holiday season. Many people volunteer their time or make donations to the less fortunate. Collecting gifts for children's toy drives, food for Christmas hampers, or warm clothing during the cold winter months are all ways to contribute.

Pages 20–21

Special music is played to celebrate the holiday season. Christmas music can help spread feelings of happiness and love. People enjoy singing about angels or the birth of Jesus. In some neighborhoods, people go door-to-door singing Christmas carols. There are many non-religious Christmas songs as well, celebrating festive figures such as Rudolph the Red-nosed Reindeer or Frosty the Snowman.

KEY WORDS

Research has shown that as much as 65 percent of all written material published in English is made up of 300 words. These 300 words cannot be taught using pictures or learned by sounding them out. They must be recognized by sight. This book contains 65 common sight words to help young readers improve their reading fluency and comprehension. This book also teaches young readers several important content words, such as proper nouns. These words are paired with pictures to aid in learning and improve understanding.

Page	Sight Words First Appearance
4	a, before, day, every, is, it, of, on, the, to, year
6	about, been, for, has
7	also, by, from, just, not, other, people, that, they, was
8	an, and, around, at, children, good, he, homes, important, leaves, plays, world
11	are, in, many, place, take
12	as, ones, only, think, time, with
15	eat, foods, get, often, or, such, together
16	lights, more, than, trees
19	help, made, need, some, those
20	songs

Page	Content Words First Appearance
4	birth, Christmas, Christmas Eve, December, Jesus Christ
7	Christians, customs, God, holiday, son, traditions, winter festivals
8	presents, role, Santa Claus
11	celebrations, church services, Peoria, Illinois, Santa Claus Parade, United States
12	holiday
15	fruitcake, meal, shortbread cookies, stuffing, treats, turkey
16	Christmas trees, New York City, ornaments, Rockefeller Center, symbol
19	clothing, donations, gifts, toys
20	carols, music, season

Published by Smartbook Media Inc.
350 5th Avenue, 59th Floor New York, NY 10118
Website: www.openlightbox.com

Library of Congress Control Number: 2019939941

ISBN 978-1-5105-4500-7 (hardcover)
ISBN 978-1-5105-4501-4 (multi-user eBook)

042019
122918

Printed in Guangzhou, China
1 2 3 4 5 6 7 8 9 0 23 22 21 20 19

Project Coordinator: Priyanka Das
Art Director: Terry Paulhus

Every reasonable effort has been made to trace ownership and to obtain permission to reprint copyright material. The publisher would be pleased to have any errors or omissions brought to its attention so that they may be corrected in subsequent printings.

The publisher acknowledges Getty Images, iStock, Corbis, and Shutterstock as its primary image suppliers for this title.